SUPER CITIES!

The TWIN CITIES

by Colleen Sexton

arcadia®
CHILDREN'S BOOKS

Published by Arcadia Children's Books
A Division of Arcadia Publishing
Charleston, SC
www.arcadiapublishing.com

First published 2022

Manufactured in the United States.

ISBN 978-1-4671-9857-8

Library of Congress Control Number: 2021943356

Produced by Shoreline Publishing Group LLC
Santa Barbara, California
Designer: Patty Kelley

Contents

WELCOME TO The Twin Cities

FAST FACTS

Minneapolis, Minnesota

POPULATION: 433,000

FOUNDED: 1854

AREA: 54 Square Miles

Look at the center of a map of the United States. Now go north. A little farther. Right at the top is Minnesota. That northern state's largest cities are Minneapolis and St. Paul. They're so close together that they're known as the Twin Cities! (To locals, they're just "The Cities.")

They might be "twins," but Minneapolis and St. Paul are very different cities. Minneapolis features a busy downtown with modern skyscrapers. Trendy neighborhoods draw crowds to its

FAST FACTS

St. Paul, Minnesota

POPULATION:
307,000

FOUNDED:
1867

AREA:
52 Square Miles

shops and restaurants. Minneapolis is also a hub for sports and the arts. St. Paul, the state's capital city, is a bit smaller and quieter. It's a welcoming city with a historic feel. Both cities have a lot to offer—it just depends what you're looking for!

This book will explore the people and places that make Minneapolis and St. Paul great places to live and to visit. Let's go to the Twin Cities!

TWIN CITIES: Map 'em!

Where do great cities grow up? Near great rivers! Minneapolis and its eastern neighbor, St. Paul, both stand along the mighty Mississippi River. The waterway cuts southeast through downtown Minneapolis, creating a West bank and an East bank. The river then flows near the border with St. Paul. The Minnesota River rolls in from the southwest, meeting the Mississippi as it bends east to wind through St. Paul. From the Twin Cities, the Mississippi River continues its long journey south to the Gulf of Mexico.

Minneapolis-St. Paul, Minnesota
N
Mississippi River
Minneapolis
St. Paul
Chain of Lakes
Mississippi River
Minnesota River
Minneapolis city limits
St. Paul city limits

THE MEANING OF MINNEAPOLIS

Minneapolis almost had a different name. In 1852, officials selected the name All Saints. Enter local teacher and farmer Charles Hoag. He found the name meaningless and decided he could do better.

Hoag suggested the name Minnehapolis in a letter to the local newspaper. He chose the word *minnehaha*, meaning "laughing waters" in the Dakota language (the Dakota people were the first to live in the area; see page 16). He combined it with *polis*, the Greek word for "city." Hoag noted that the *h* would be silent.

Charles Hoag

Hoag's idea was a hit. The newspaper's editor, George A. Bowman, declared the name "excellent" and "admirably descriptive of the locality." He also called the silent *h* "poetic." On this last point, the citizens disagreed. They accepted the name but dropped the *h*. Without that letter, the name *Minneapolis* means "water city."

THE CITY OF LAKES

The state of Minnesota is known as the Land of 10,000 Lakes. With 22 of them in Minneapolis, it's no wonder that one of the city's nicknames is the City of Lakes!

Five of the largest lakes form the popular Chain of Lakes. Each lake has its own personality. Residents visit some lakes to swim, picnic, or catch a concert. Other lakes are quiet places to enjoy nature.

The Chain of Lakes draws visitors year-round. In summer, colorful sailboats glide across the water. Kayakers and paddle boarders explore the shoreline. Winter brings out iceboaters and cross-country skiers. Pond hockey players hit the ice for a pick-up game. In all kinds of weather, walkers, joggers, and bikers enjoy the 15 miles of paved trails that circle the lakes.

FAST FACT

Bde Maka Ska got its name from the Dakota language. It's pronounced "buh-DAY muh-KAH skah."

Snow yoga—snowga!

The Chain of Lakes

Lake Harriet
Bde Maka Ska (formerly Lake Calhoun)
Lake of the Isles
Cedar Lake
Brownie Lake

The Elf Door: In 1995, an elf moved his family into an ash tree near Lake Harriet. It became their summer home. The elf installed a wooden door with a lion's head door knocker. Sharp-eyed residents spotted the door while strolling along the lakeshore. Kids began leaving notes for the elf, stuffing them inside his wee door. And he wrote back! His responses came on little cards in tiny type signed "Mr. Little Guy." Every summer, he answers thousands of notes. Over the years, residents have learned a few things about Mr. Little Guy. He likes to dance the samba, he enjoys minnow pizza, and he's an ElfBall fan!

FROM PIG'S EYE TO ST. PAUL

St. Paul's name begins with Pierre Parrant, the first person of European descent to settle where the city now stands. Because of a missing eye, he wore an eye patch, and he was known as "Pig's Eye." Parrant was a shady character and a bootlegger, someone who illegally made and sold liquor. In 1838, he set up shop at Fountain Cave along the Mississippi River.

Pierre Parrant

Parrant's tavern, called Pig's Eye, became popular with visitors and nearby residents. A local man mailed a letter using "Pig's Eye" as the return address. The name stuck, and the growing community became known as Pig's Eye.

Lucien Galtier

In 1841, a newly arrived Catholic priest named Lucien Galtier built a small log church that he named for Saint Paul. Disturbed by the name Pig's Eye, Galtier convinced residents to rename the community for the church. When the city was established in 1854, the name St. Paul became official.

Cathedral of St. Paul

THE CAPITAL CITY

St. Paul is Minnesota's capital city and home to one of the country's most beautiful state capitol buildings. In 1895, officials held a competition to design the capitol. The winning entry came from local architect Cass Gilbert. On a July day in 1898, marching bands led a huge crowd to the highest point in downtown St. Paul. They had a ceremony to lay the capitol's cornerstone, which signals the start of construction. A gleaming white marble building featuring a dome, columns, and arches rose on the site. Completed in 1905, it became the center of Minnesota's government.

Visitors can explore Minnesota's history through more than 150 works of art inside the capitol.

The site of celebrations and protests, the broad capitol grounds are known as "Minnesota's front lawn."

A shining gold sculpture known as the Quadriga sits at the base of the capitol's dome. It features a chariot pulled by four horses.

The capitol has the second largest unsupported marble dome in the world. (The first is St. Peter's Basilica in Vatican City and the third is the Taj Majal in India.)

The Architect: Cass Gilbert grew up in St. Paul. He designed the Minnesota State Capitol and supervised all details of its construction, inside and out. This work made him a national celebrity. Gilbert went on to design the U.S. Supreme Court Building in Washington, D.C., and two other state capitols. His most famous work is the Woolworth Building in New York City, one of the country's first skyscrapers.

HISTORY: Early Days

For at least 10,000 years, people have traveled Minnesota's lakes and rivers. By the 1600s, the Dakota people made their home in the area that is now the Twin Cities. They called it Bdote, meaning "where two rivers come together." The Ojibwe people, who lived in northern Minnesota, often traveled to Bdote to trade furs and other goods. The place where the Minnesota and Mississippi Rivers meet came to be an important gathering place for both peoples.

When the ice froze each winter, the Dakota people took to the lakes and rivers to play ball. They used sticks with nets on the end, similar to the modern-day sport of lacrosse.

About 2,000 years ago, the Hopewell people built burial mounds on a bluff overlooking the Mississippi River. The Dakota people later used the same burial ground. Along with their dead, the Dakota people buried valuable items such as knives, pipes, and even canoes.

Dakota women were known for their detailed beadwork. They shaped shells, stones, bones, and teeth into beads to sew onto clothing, bags, and other items. Later, the Dakota people offered food and animal skins to European traders in exchange for glass beads.

The Dakota people lived on Minnesota meadows like this one.

The Ojibwe and Dakota peoples traveled lakes and rivers in birch bark canoes. They fit sheets of birch bark over a wooden frame made of cedar or spruce. The canoes were light enough for one person to carry, yet strong enough to go over dangerous rapids.

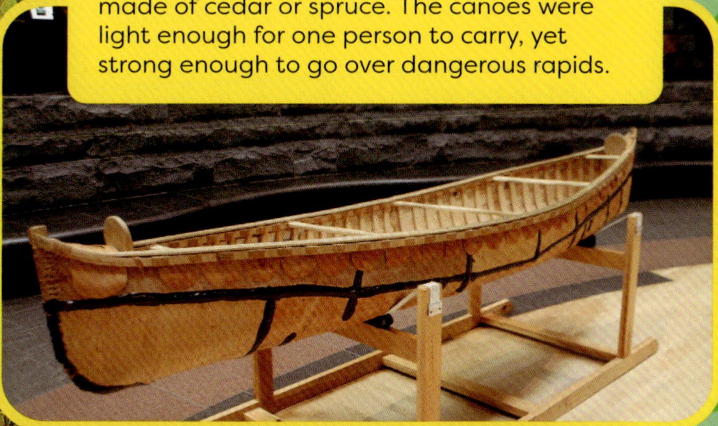

HISTORY: Early Days

1680: While paddling up the Mississippi River, French missionary and explorer Father Louis Hennepin was captured by Dakota warriors. During his peaceful four months with the Dakota, Hennepin saw the only true waterfall on the Mississippi River in what is now Minneapolis. After his release and return to Europe, he wrote about his "discovery," which he named St. Anthony Falls.

1819: The US Army established Fort Snelling on a bluff high above where the Mississippi and Minnesota Rivers meet. Completed in 1825, it became a hub for soldiers, their families, government officials, and fur traders. Although it was illegal, some officers and government officials kept enslaved people here. The fort also drew settlers from eastern U.S. states. The Dakota and Ojibwe peoples continued to live and trade in the area.

1837: The Ojibwe and Dakota peoples signed a treaty giving up their lands east of the Mississippi River in exchange for money, goods, and hunting rights. It wasn't long before settlers put pressure on the government to make more land available. In an 1851 treaty, the Dakota people were forced to move onto reservations in western Minnesota.

1830s: Steamboats started chugging up the Mississippi River to St. Paul, where they delivered trade goods, mail, soldiers, and settlers. For some travelers, St. Paul was a welcome place to outfit themselves for a long journey west. The city quickly grew into a commercial center and became the capital of the Minnesota Territory in 1849. (Minnesota officially became a state in 1858.)

1850: St. Anthony Falls fueled the development of Minneapolis. The falls powered sawmills, providing work for thousands of lumberjacks. Farmers brought wheat to flour mills built along the falls (which used milling stones like this one). Soon Minneapolis became the flour-milling capital of the world, earning the nickname Mill City.

HISTORY: Late 1800s

1861–1865: Fort Snelling served as a training center for soldiers during the Civil War. Minnesota's regiments fought in battles across the South. Fort Snelling processed more than 25,000 soldiers as they returned home.

1869: Charles A. Pillsbury bought into a struggling flour business on the Mississippi River. He installed advanced equipment in his mills that revolutionized the flour business. Pillsbury also hired an architect to design a new mill that in 1882 became the largest mill in the world.

1882: The nation's first hydroelectric power station began operating in Minneapolis just below St. Anthony Falls. Machines connected to a waterwheel sent power to overhead wires along Washington Avenue. The wires carried power to light up businesses in the area.

1889: Speedy travel arrived when electric streetcars began running in the Twin Cities. New lines were added quickly. Soon residents could hop on and ride all the way from Minneapolis to St. Paul. The use of electric streetcars peaked in 1920 when 900 cars ran on 523 miles of track. Until it finally closed in 1954 because so many people were driving cars, the system was considered one of the best in the country.

1917: The Minnesota State Fair in St. Paul became a "food training camp" as a way to help boost the nation's food supply during World War I. It featured new machines, new farming methods, and new varieties of corn and wheat that would increase the harvest. The fair also offered classes in gardening, canning, and cooking to help home cooks deal with food shortages.

HISTORY: The Twin Cities Grow Up

1929: The Foshay Tower was completed, rising more than 447 feet in downtown Minneapolis. At the time, it was the tallest building between Chicago and the Pacific coast. The Foshay Tower remained Minneapolis's tallest skyscraper until 1973.

1930: St. Paul was a "crooks' haven." Gangsters, bootleggers, and bank robbers slipped into the city to hide from the law. Among these infamous criminals were mob boss Al "Scarface" Capone and bank robber John Dillinger (right, otherwise known as "public enemy number one"). St. Paul experienced kidnappings, shootouts, and robberies before its "gangster era" came to an end in 1936.

1956: Construction began on Interstate-94, a highway that would connect downtown Minneapolis with downtown St. Paul. Its route greatly affected the Rondo neighborhood, home to half of St. Paul's Black citizens. A strong, thriving community, Rondo protested the construction. In the end, however, Interstate-94 took 600 of Rondo's homes and cut the neighborhood in two.

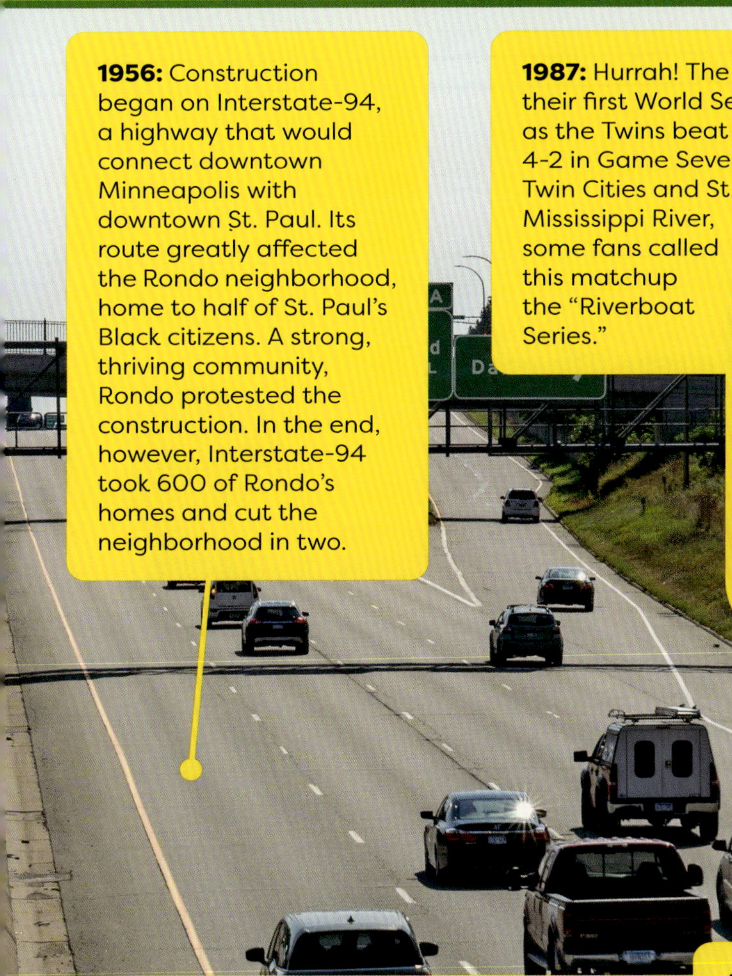

1987: Hurrah! The Minnesota Twins won their first World Series. The crowd roared as the Twins beat the St. Louis Cardinals 4-2 in Game Seven. Noting that the Twin Cities and St. Louis both sat on the Mississippi River, some fans called this matchup the "Riverboat Series."

August 1, 2007: The Interstate-35 West bridge collapsed over the Mississippi River in Minneapolis during peak rush hour. A beam broke and a large section of the bridge fell into the river, killing 13 people and injuring 145. The cause was an unknown design flaw in the bridge, which had been built more than 40 years earlier.

BLACK LIVES MATTER

On May 25, 2020, the nation turned its attention to Minneapolis. An unarmed Black man named George Floyd was accused of using a fake $20 bill in a store. The police came, handcuffed Floyd, and forced him to the ground where officer Derek Chauvin knelt on his neck and back for nine minutes and 29 seconds.

Floyd repeatedly asked for help and said "I can't breathe." Three other officers helped pin Floyd down and keep witnesses away. Floyd died on the street. One witness recorded the incident on video, which quickly went viral.

Floyd's death sparked protests against police brutality. Over several nights, thousands of people in the Twin Cities came together to protest peacefully. They carried signs saying "Black Lives Matter," "Stop Police Brutality," and "Justice for George Floyd." But there was a lot of anger. Some protests became violent, and people destroyed property, set fires, and looted stores. The Twin Cities were in chaos. The governor activated the National Guard to help protect residents, businesses, and peaceful protesters. The protests in the Twin Cities inspired a movement against police brutality and racial inequality across the country and around the world. About a year later, Derek Chauvin was convicted of murder and sentenced to 22 years in prison. A memorial arose in the place where George Floyd was killed. It's now called George Floyd Square.

People from the Past!

Meet just a few of the interesting people in Twin Cities history.

Seth Eastman (1808–1875)
A mapmaker and illustrator for the US Army, Eastman was also a painter whose works showed Native American peoples as they really lived. While stationed at Fort Snelling, he painted scenes of the Dakota and Ojibwe people hunting, canoeing, and setting up camps. Eastman later designed the Minnesota territorial seal.

James J. Hill (1838–1916)
At age 17, Hill arrived in St. Paul to seek his fortune. After 20 years in the shipping business, he became an owner of what would be the Great Northern Railway. The rail line would run north to Canada and west to the Pacific coast. Over time, Hill bought other railroads and dabbled in banking, mining, and agriculture. His great success earned him the nickname Empire Builder. His home, called James J. Hill House, is open for tours.

Gratia Alta Countryman (1866–1953)

As the director of the Minneapolis Public Library, Countryman wanted to bring books to "the faraway corners of the city." She set up reading rooms in fire halls, factories, and hospitals. In the central library, she opened the nation's first children's section. Countryman's ideas spread across the nation when she was elected president of the American Library Association in 1934.

FAST FACT

In 1971, three student teachers in Minneapolis created a game called Oregon Trail to teach students about westward migration. Back then, kids played the game on a teletype machine. Today, millions still play it—on their phones!

Marcenia Lyle "Toni" Stone (1921–1996)

Nicknamed "Tomboy," Stone grew up playing baseball in the Rondo neighborhood of St. Paul. At 16, she joined the Twin City Colored Giants and then played for teams in the Negro Minor League. Stone made history as the first woman to play in the Negro Leagues. In 1953, she signed a contract with the Indianapolis Clowns.

THE TWIN CITIES TODAY

The Twin Cities have grown into bustling cities where residents share a love of the arts and the outdoors. Here are a few things Minneapolis and St. Paul are known for.

Parks: Nearly everyone in Minneapolis and St. Paul lives only a 10-minute walk away from a park. The two cities regularly top the list of the best park systems in the country.

Biking: With 98 miles of bike lanes and 101 miles of off-street trails, Minneapolis is known as one of the best biking cities in the country. About 20,000 residents commute by bike during the summer, while about 7,000 commute year-round—yes, even in winter!

Minnehaha Park, home to Minnehaha Falls

Live Theater: Bravo! Twin Cities residents enjoy live performances in more than 200 theaters, including the Guthrie Theater, the largest regional playhouse in the country. The Twin Cities is the nation's third-largest live theater market after New York City and Chicago.

Golf: Fore! Minneapolis has more golfers per capita than any other city in the country. Residents love golf so much that they buy colored golf balls and play in the snow!

The TWIN CITIES for Everyone

Native American Peoples

More than 35,000 Native American people live in the Twin Cities area, one of the country's largest urban Native American populations. Many make their homes in the Franklin Avenue and Phillips neighborhoods of Minneapolis, which have been named the American Indian Cultural Corridor. Today, this area has become a place where residents and visitors can enjoy Native American culture, food, and art. This area is also home to the Minneapolis American Indian Center, which offers health services, youth programs, and community gathering spaces.

The American Swedish Institute helps connect Minnesotans with their roots.

Scandinavians

Scandinavian roots run deep in Minnesota. In the late 1800s, thousands of Norwegian and Swedish immigrants began forming tight-knit communities in the Twin Cities. They found jobs in the railroad, flour-milling, textile, and lumber industries. With skill and experience in working with their hands, Scandinavian workers were in demand. Politicians Hubert Humphrey and Walter Mondale, both sons of Norwegian immigrants, rose to the office of vice president of the United States. Today, the Scandinavian influence is still going strong, from traditional foods to art museums to the name of the state's professional football team (Go Vikings!).

Black Americans

The Black community in the Twin Cities began growing in the 1800s and 1900s. Many freed enslaved people found safety in Minnesota. But like in other cities around the country, they also found discrimination. Black families were often prevented from working in certain jobs or living in certain neighborhoods. So they created their own thriving neighborhoods where they built churches, started community centers, and established Black business districts. They also published a number of newspapers. Founded in 1934, the *Minnesota Spokesman-Recorder* is the state's oldest Black newspaper and longest running Black-owned business.

People from Mexico

The Latinx community in the Twin Cities started growing in the early 1900s. Immigrants mostly from Mexico headed north to find work, especially in the stockyards and factories. Many families settled in St. Paul's West Side neighborhood where they found support and community at Our Lady of Guadalupe Roman Catholic Church. By the mid-1900s, the West Side was a thriving Mexican-American community. Businesses continue to open in the area known as District del Sol, which holds one of the country's largest Cinco de Mayo celebrations each year.

Hmong Community

An ethnic group with roots in China, Hmong refugees began arriving in Minnesota from the war-torn country of Laos in 1975. Today, more than 76,000 Hmong people live in the Twin Cities. Early immigrants focused on providing English education and job training to newcomers. Some started farming projects and still sell their harvests at Twin Cities farmers markets. New generations in the Hmong community entered business and politics. The heart of the Hmong community is in the Frogtown neighborhood of St. Paul, home to Hmong restaurants, businesses, a large indoor marketplace, and the Hmong Cultural Center.

People from Somalia

In the early 1990s, refugees fleeing civil war in the East African nation of Somalia came to the Twin Cities. Today, the Somali population numbers more than 60,000. The Somali people built a strong community in the Cedar-Riverside neighborhood of Minneapolis. They joined together to keep their African cultural traditions and Muslim religious traditions alive while starting lives in a new country. It wasn't easy. Most Somali people practice the Muslim religion, and faced discrimination. But the Somali community has grown and thrived. Minneapolis has many Somali shops and restaurants, a mosque, a Somali history museum, and the Karmel Mall, a marketplace that features dozens of Somali-run businesses.

FAST FACT

In 2019, Somali native Ilhan Omar was elected to represent part of Minneapolis in the United States House of Representatives. She is the first Somali American to be a congressperson.

Seasons in the Cities

Twin Cities Climate and Weather

When is the best time to visit the Twin Cities? That depends—what kind of weather do you like? With four seasons and a wild mix of weather, there's a best time of year for everyone.

Winter

How cold are winters in the Twin Cities? *Brr...*they're cold! Temperatures stay below freezing on most days, and sometimes they dip well below zero. The first snowfall usually arrives in November. By the end of winter, the snow total is usually more than 50 inches. Winter can get dangerous when blizzards strike. These storms bring strong winds and heavy snow.

FAST FACT

The largest blizzard to affect the Twin Cities started on Halloween in 1991. It snowed for three days, dumping more than 28 inches of snow!

Spring

March brings signs of spring. The days slowly get warmer as temperatures rise above freezing. The snow melts to slush. By April, the high temperatures are above 40°F. It finally feels like spring when the snow is gone, the grass is green, and there are buds on the trees in early May. Spring also brings thunderstorms and the start of tornado season.

Summer

Leaves open on trees and flowers bloom. Summers in the Twin Cities can be warm, pleasant, and sunny. They can also be hot and humid, with temperatures rising well above 90°F. The area sometimes experiences droughts. Other times, heavy thunderstorms can lead to flash flooding.

Fall

September brings cooler temperatures. The Twin Cities enjoy crisp fall days with bright blue skies. By October, trees blaze with yellow, orange, and red leaves. By November, it's cold again and time to dig out the winter coats!

St. Anthony Falls

Visit the only waterfall on the Mississippi River. Take a guided tour onto the lock walls to learn how the falls shaped the city and its mill industry. And get some great views from the Third Street Bridge that soars above the falls.

Things to see in the Twin Cities

Minneapolis

Stone Arch Bridge

This bridge with its 23 arches spans the Mississippi River just south of St. Anthony Falls. Until 1965 it was a railroad bridge. Today, walkers and bikers use the bridge. Take a stroll across and enjoy views of the river, the falls, and the Minneapolis skyline.

Midtown Global Market

Experience new sights, flavors, and sounds! Join the more than 1.5 million people each year who visit the Midtown Global Market. This cultural center is home to more than 45 businesses that span more than 22 cultures. Check out the shops and the wide variety of restaurants. The market also offers arts and crafts, music, and dance programs.

Lyndale Park

Follow the winding paths in this beautiful park to explore its gardens. The Peace Garden features a zigzag bridge and a peace crane sculpture. At its summer peak, more than 60,000 blooms cover the Rose Garden. The Annual and Perennial Garden forms a long border of colorful flowers.

Things to see in the Twin Cities

St. Paul

Como Park Conservatory

The "jewel in the crown" of the Conservatory is a glass-domed garden that dates to 1915 (left). The gardens include orchids, ferns, bonsai, and tropical flowers. The Japanese Garden is world famous. The Conservatory also hosts flower shows, concerts, and classes.

Mickey's Diner

Opened in 1939, this railroad car diner is somewhat of a star. It's appeared on TV, in movies, and in magazines. For locals, it's the place to get a delicious breakfast anytime. Mickey's has been operated by three generations of the same family.

Summit Avenue

Summit Avenue is a five-mile stretch of grand Victorian homes, the longest in the country. There are 373 homes in all. They include railroad tycoon James J. Hill's home, which offers tours.

GETTING AROUND THE TWIN CITIES

Twin Cities residents travel mainly by car, bus, and bicycle. But a few more options have popped up in recent years. Here are some other ways residents get around.

Trains: Light Rail serves much of downtown Minneapolis and connects to St. Paul. It also has a line that runs to the airport and the Mall of America.

eScooters: These electric two-wheelers go up to 15 miles per hour. They can be rented via an app.

Skyways: Enclosed walkways link buildings in the downtown areas of Minneapolis and St. Paul. Altogether, the Twin Cities has nearly 15 miles of skyways! They help residents stay warm in winter and cool in summer.

eBikes: Commuters can also use an app to rent ebikes called "Nice Ride." Pedaling starts a motor that helps riders get where they're going in less time.

IT'S OFFICIAL!

Minneapolis and St. Paul each have their own official symbols. So does the state of Minnesota! Check them out!

OFFICIAL MINNEAPOLIS FLAG:

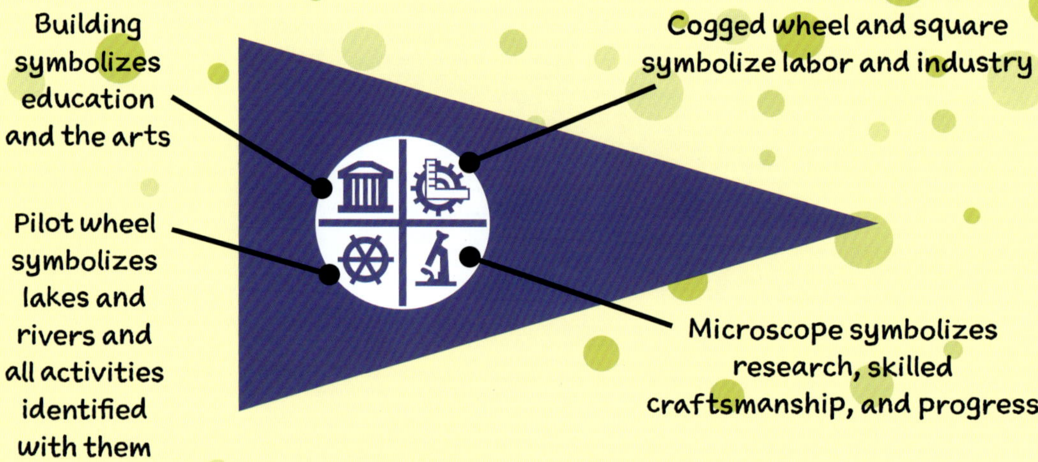

OFFICIAL ST. PAUL FLAG:

OFFICIAL BEE:
Rusty-patched bumble bee

OFFICIAL MINNESOTA STUFF

Fish: walleye

Fruit: honeycrisp apple

Tree: Norway Pine

Mushroom: morel

Sport: hockey

Muffin: blueberry

Drink: milk

Grain: wild rice

OFFICIAL FLOWER:
Pink Lady's Slipper

OFFICIAL GEMSTONE:
Agate

OFFICIAL BIRD:
Loon

OFFICIAL BUTTERFLY:
Monarch

Minneapolis Sculpture Garden:
An 11-acre park featuring more than 40 works of art, including the famous Spoon Bridge and Cherry sculpture.
Created by Claes Oldenburg and Coosje van Bruggen

Art in the Twin Cities

The Twin Cities is a creative community. Outdoor art livens up a neighborhood and brings people together. Here are just a few of the outdoor murals and sculptures that grace Twin Cities neighborhoods.

Outdoor Art in Minneapolis

The Times They Are A-Changin: A three-part mural that shows musician Bob Dylan (born in Minnesota!) at three stages of his career.

The Globe Mural: This work on the Theatre in the Round uses *trompe l'oeil*, a painted technique that creates a 3-D effect.

Prince Murals: Several paintings honor the ground-breaking musician, who died in 2016. This one is in Chanhassen, the Minneapolis surburb where he grew up.

Outdoor Art in Minneapolis

More from Minneapolis Sculpture Garden: The Garden was opened in 1988 and completely redesigned in 2017. Millions of people visit each year!

"Hahn/Cock" by Katharina Fritsch

"Hare on Bell on Portland Stone Piers" by Barry Flanagan

"The Spinner" by Alexander Calder

"Arikidea" by Mark di Suvero

Outdoor Art in St. Paul

Western Sculpture Park: Kids can touch, climb, and run around the sculptures in this park

Skygate: A stainless steel and acrylic work inspired by ice palaces and gateways

Minneapolis Museums

From art to history to science, Twin Cities museums have something for everyone. Here are some to discover.

Minneapolis Institute of Art: This popular museum is home to more than 80,000 objects and is one of the country's largest art museums. Works range from ancient sculptures to modern photography. Its special exhibits always draw big crowds.

Walker Art Center: This museum is known worldwide for its fine collection of contemporary and modern art. With 11 galleries, there is a lot to explore. The museum also hosts film screenings and performances in its two theaters.

Weisman Art Museum: Teaching is the main mission of this museum located on the University of Minnesota campus. Its exhibits explain how artworks fit into history and culture. The museum holds a large collection of twentieth-century American art.

Bakken Museum: This museum celebrates electricity in many forms. Play electronic instruments, create a stop-motion movie, and step into a phone booth to learn about communication. Page through a magic book to bring a science fiction story to life. Also explore the science of Mary Shelley's novel *Frankenstein*. Make one of her characters come to life in a puppet theater.

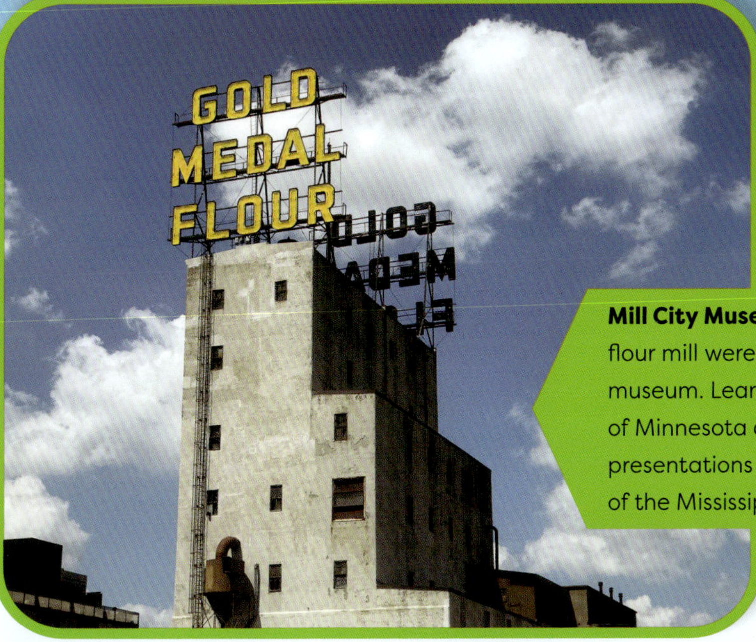

Mill City Museum: The ruins of a flour mill were transformed into a museum. Learn about the history of Minnesota and its mills through presentations and walking tours of the Mississippi riverfront.

St. Paul Museums

Minnesota Children's Museum: This is the place to play! Climb four stories up the Scramble and whoosh down on a spiral slide. Paint on a canvas or a wall. Hop across a river of hot lava or creep through a laser maze. Head outside to taste, touch, and smell plants. Explore the light with a giant kaleidoscope.

Science Museum of Minnesota: There's so much to explore at this museum! See fossils of giant dinosaurs, create a tornado, visit an Egyptian mummy, and see what it's like to captain a river towboat. Catch a film at the Omnitheater to watch science come to life on a huge domed screen.

Bell Museum of Natural History: Explore the story of life, beginning with the formation of the universe at the planetarium. Learn about Minnesota's prehistoric past. See how the state's wildlife and ecosystems have changed over time through amazingly realistic dioramas. Don't miss the wooly mammoth!

Minnesota History Center: Explore Minnesota's past and learn about the people and events that shaped the state. Step inside a tipi to learn about Dakota history and culture. Try hauling a fur trader's pack. Visit a sod house to learn about life on the prairie. Hop on a wagon loaded with grain for market. And that's just one of many exhibits!

The World Comes to the Twin Cities

The Twin Cities welcomes people from all over the world. These places celebrate their cultures.

◀ **American Swedish Institute:** Swedish immigrant Swan Turnblad, who rose from a typesetter to a newspaper publisher, built this 33-room mansion in 1903. Today, it is dedicated to the history of Swedish culture in the Twin Cities. The Institute hosts exhibits, events, and festivals.

▼ **Hmong Cultural Center:** The center keeps Hmong culture alive through classes in music, dance, ceremonial arts, and Hmong history. It also holds a large collection of Hmong-related literature. New immigrants can access support to learn English, find jobs, and become U.S. citizens.

◀ Somali Museum of Minnesota: This museum invites the community to learn about traditional Somali arts. It displays more than 700 objects and offers educational programs that aim to keep young Somali-Americans connected to their culture.

➤ Museum of Russian Art: With a collection of more than 7,000 works, this is North America's only museum dedicated to Russian culture. The museum also hosts speakers and concerts.

Jewish Historical Society of the Upper Midwest: This historical society preserves photographs and films, family histories, synagogue records, and scrapbooks. The collection tells the story of Jews who arrived in the area as immigrants, farmers, and business owners nearly 200 years ago.

Performing Arts

The Twin Cities is known as a center for the arts. Audiences fill venues large and small. Here are some of the best-known and most popular places to see live performances.

The **Minnesota Opera** has been delivering pitch-perfect performances for more than 55 years. Its performance home is the Ordway Center for the performing arts.

Big names in the Twin Cities theater scene include the **Guthrie Theater**, **Orpheum Theatre**, **State Theatre**, **Pantages Theatre**, **Fitzgerald Theater**, **Children's Theatre Company**, and the **Ordway Center for the Performing Arts**. These venues host plays and musicals that bring audiences to their feet!

Theater roots run deep in the Twin Cities. Smaller venues draw audiences for locally produced plays, musicals, and festivals. They include the **Jungle Theater**, **Mixed Blood Theatre**, **Illusion Theater, Theatre in the Round**, and the **Southern Theater**.

The Twin Cities Ballet performs original productions of classic stories. Its annual production of A Minnesota Nutcracker Ballet is a holiday tradition that draws thousands of fans.

First Avenue is the center for live music in the Twin Cities. This legendary music club launched the careers of Prince, the Replacements, Lizzo (below), and many other artists.

The **Minnesota Orchestra** brings a wide variety of classical music to audiences across the state and around the world. Classical music fans also enjoy performances by the **Metropolitan Symphony Orchestra** and the **St. Paul Chamber Orchestra**.

How to Talk Twin Cities

Minnesotans have their own way of saying things. Here are a few words and phrases that will help you talk like the locals.

Ope!

Means "oops!" Usually used when you bump into someone.

The Cities

What everyone in Minnesota calls Minneapolis and St. Paul.

"That's different" or "That's interesting"

What to say when you don't want to give your opinion or you think your opinion might be impolite.

Uff da!

Means "oh!" It's usually used when you feel relieved, surprised, or tired out

pop

Not soda or soda pop.

hotdish

Meat, vegetables, and canned soup baked together in a pan. Tater tots often top a hotdish. Other people might call it a casserole.

Up North

The place where there are a lot of lakes and cabins. Since lakes and cabins are everywhere, it means any place in the state that's north of where you are.

THE TWIN CITIES: They're Weird!

It's a Revolution!

A Minneapolis restaurant called Betty Dangers Animal Farm features a revolving patio—a vertical revolving patio. Nicknamed "The Revolution" (right), the patio looks like a Ferris wheel. People can enjoy a meal in a dining car as the patio goes around. The Revolution is open year-round, so diners need to bundle up in the winter!

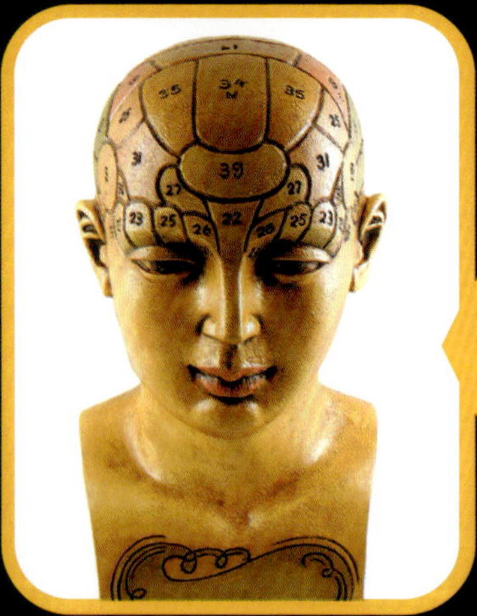

Questionable Indeed!

The Science Museum of Minnesota has a Questionable Medical Devices collection. These old-time gadgets were once taken seriously. One of the weirdest devices is a phrenology reader. This machine measures bumps on people's heads to determine their personalities.

Lite It Up!

Union Depot in St. Paul is home to the world's largest Lite Brite picture. At 12 feet by 24 feet, it holds more than 596,000 Lite Brite pegs. More than 600 volunteers helped put together the mural's abstract design. What a bright idea!

No Kitten!

Thousands of cat lovers and lovers of internet cat videos get together for the Cat Video Festival. The crowd, many wearing cat ears, laugh and cheer at the cat antics on the big screen. The St. Paul Saints host this annual event at CHS Field. (Sorry, no actual cats allowed in the ballpark!)

Popular People

Charles M. Schulz

Prince

Charles M. Schulz
St. Paul is the hometown of this famous cartoonist. In 1950, he introduced Charlie Brown, Snoopy, and the rest of the Peanuts gang to the country. Today, statues of his characters dot the city. You never know where you might run into one!

Prince Rogers Nelson was a native of Minneapolis and a music legend. As a kid, he taught himself to play piano, guitar, and a bunch of other instruments. He later led the way in creating the "Minneapolis Sound" of the 1980s, a blend of rock, pop, funk, blues, and punk music. A singer, songwriter, and musician, Prince sold more than 100 million albums and won seven Grammy Awards.

Louise Erdrich

Erdrich started writing stories at an early age and never stopped. Her books for both adults and children are inspired by her Native American ancestry. Erdrich won the National Book Award for her novel *The Round House* and the Pulitzer Prize for *The Night Watchman*. Her books for children include The Birchbark House series. Erdrich owns Birchbark Books, an independent bookstore in Minneapolis.

Suni Lee

At the Summer Olympics in Tokyo in 2021, gymnast Suni Lee jumped and flipped her way to gold as the all-around champion. She also took home silver in the team final and bronze on the uneven bars. Lee, who grew up in St. Paul, is the first Hmong-American Olympian.

What People Do in the TWIN CITIES

About 3.2 million people live in the Twin Cities area. Here are some of the common industries they work in.

Large retail companies Target and Best Buy have headquarters in the area. Thousands of people work for them in a variety of jobs.

So many global leaders in the healthcare industry are based in Minnesota that it has earned the nickname Medical Alley. Major employers in the Twin Cities area include 3M, Medtronic, Ecolab, and United Healthcare.

The Twin Cities is the financial center of the upper midwest. Banks, finance companies, and insurance companies are important to the area. Minneapolis is also home to the Ninth Federal Reserve District Bank.

The Twin Cities area has one of the country's largest high-tech communities. Scientists and engineers do research and train at the University of Minnesota and other colleges in the area.

Manufacturing is big business in the Twin Cities area. Workers make a wide variety of products, including electronics, food and dairy products, supercomputers, and electronic medical equipment.

Eat the Twin Cities Way

Twin Cities residents enjoy foods from a variety of cultures, but there are some traditional foods that are uniquely Minnesotan.

The Jucy Lucy Take two thin hamburger patties and pinch them together around a hunk of cheese. Grill it up to create a melted cheese center and you have the famous Jucy Lucy. This burger is at the center of a delicious feud between Matt's Bar and the 5-8 Club. They both claim to have invented Minneapolis's signature burger in the 1950s.

Wild Rice The Ojibwe people traditionally harvested wild rice on lakes and waterways. It has a nutty flavor and a chewy texture. Over the years, it became an ingredient in many Minnesota dishes. Chicken wild rice soup is a favorite!

Walleye Caught in lakes around the state, walleye is Minnesota's favorite fish. The sweet, mild fish works well in many dishes. Some favorites include walleye sandwiches, walleye cakes, beer-battered walleye, and walleye tacos. Many local chefs even have signature walleye dishes.

Honeycrisp Apples The honeycrisp is a juicy, crunchy apple with just the right balance of sweet and tart. It's good for eating and for baking. Developed by the University of Minnesota, the honeycrisp was introduced in 1991. Some call it America's favorite apple!

Scandinavian Favorites Many traditional Minnesota foods have Scandinavian roots. The Norwegian dish *lefse* is a flat potato bread topped with butter and cinnamon sugar before rolling it up. Pickled herring is usually served with crackers. Swedish meatballs are made with both ground pork and ground beef and served in a creamy sauce. Only the brave try Lutefisk, a dish based on codfish soaked in lye.

Go, Minnesota Sports!

Minnesota is home to some awesome pro sports teams, all based in the Twin Cities. Go, team, go!

MINNESOTA VIKINGS

Joined the National Football League in 1960.

Played in four Super Bowls in the 1970s, losing each time.

Big Names: Fran Tarkenton, Randy Moss, Alan Page, Carl Eller, Adrian Peterson, Randall McDaniel, Cris Carter, Jim Marshall

Home: U.S. Bank Stadium

MINNESOTA TWINS

Joined Major League Baseball in 1961.

Won the World Series in 1987 and 1991.

Big Names: Harmon Killebrew, Kirby Puckett, Tony Oliva, Kent Hrbek, Rod Carew, Bert Blyleven, Joe Mauer

Home: Target Field

ST. PAUL SAINTS

Played baseball in independent leagues beginning in 1993. Joined the Triple-A league in 2021 with the Minnesota Twins as its parent team.

Won five league championships: 1993, 1995, 1996, 2004, 2019

Known for crazy events during games, such as the world's largest food fight and the world's largest game of Twister

Home: CHS Field

The Saints signed Ila Borders in 1997 and became the first male professional baseball team to start a female pitcher.

MINNESOTA TIMBERWOLVES

Joined the National Basketball Association in 1989

Made the playoffs eight years in a row from 1997 to 2004 and again in 2018

Big Names: Kevin Garnett, Kevin Love, Tom Gugliotta, Al Jefferson, Wally Szczerbiak, Sam Mitchell, Tony Campbell

Home: Target Center

Maya Moore

MINNESOTA LYNX

Joined the Women's National Basketball Association in 1999

Won league championships in 2011, 2013, 2015, 2017

Big Names: Maya Moore, Lindsay Whalen, Katie Smith, Seimone Agustus, Sylvia Fowles

Home: Target Center

MINNESOTA WILD

Joined the National Hockey League in 2000.

Appeared in the playoffs 11 times.

Big Names: Mikko Koivu, Marian Gaborik, Niklas Backstrom, Zach Parise, Ryan Suter

Home: Xcel Energy Center

Kirill Kaprizov scores for the Wild.

Chase Gasper

FAST FACT

The United's mascot is a loon, Minnesota's state bird.

MINNESOTA UNITED

Joined Major League Soccer in 2017

Big Names: Darwin Quintero, Christian Ramirez, Kevin Malino, Miguel Ibarra, Ethan Finlay

Home: Allianz Field

Other Sports!

Twin Cities residents like to get outdoors year-round. Here are some other ways they stay active and have fun:

So many lakes, so many **water sports**! Nothing beats being out on the water in the heat of summer. Sailboats, kayaks, canoes, and paddleboards glide across the lakes. Speed boats pull water skiers and tubers. Beaches fill with swimmers.

Biking trails crisscross the Twin Cities. One of the most popular is the Grand Rounds National Scenic Byway. Its 51 miles connect parkways throughout Minneapolis. The trail takes riders past lakes, riverbanks, wetlands, gardens, and bridges.

When temperatures drop, **hockey** lovers grab their skates and head to frozen backyard ponds and park rinks. Minneapolis even hosts the annual U.S. Pond Hockey Championships on Lake Nokomis. No wonder Minnesota is known as the State of Hockey!

Enjoy the scenery! **Hiking** trails throughout the Twin Cities wind into wooded areas and wetlands, across bridges, and along river bluffs. Hikers get amazing views of lakes, rivers, waterfalls, gardens, and cityscapes.

A lot of snow means a lot of **snow sports**! Cross-country skiers and snowshoers enjoy trails in city parks. Skiers and snowboarders hit the slopes. With every new snowfall, kids hop on their sleds and speed down neighborhood hills!

COLLEGE TOWN

From a huge university to small colleges, the Twin Cities offers great variety when it comes to education. Here are just a few schools in the Twin Cities where you might study someday!

UNIVERSITY OF MINNESOTA

Founded 1851
Students: 50,000
Popular Majors: computer science, biology, psychology, journalism, finance, education
Fast Fact: The U of M is one of the country's most respected research institutions.

UNIVERSITY OF ST. THOMAS

Founded 1885
Students: 10,000
Popular Majors: business, marketing, biology, mechanical engineering, religious studies
Fast Fact: A Catholic university, St. Thomas is the largest private university in Minnesota.

MACALESTER COLLEGE

Founded 1874
Students: 2,100
Popular Majors: economics, political science, computer science, mathematics, global studies
Fast Fact: About 60 percent of Mac students study abroad or in other U.S. cities.

MACALESTER

DUNWOODY COLLEGE OF TECHNOLOGY

Founded 1914
Students: 1,500
Popular Majors: robotics technology, construction site management, computer systems networking, automotive mechanics
Fast Fact: Dunwoody is a vocational school, meaning that it prepares students for specific jobs.

DUNWOODY
COLLEGE OF TECHNOLOGY

MINNEAPOLIS COLLEGE OF ART AND DESIGN

Founded in 1886
Students: 800
Popular Majors: illustration, animation, graphic design, painting, cinematography
Fast Fact: MCAD is one of only a few major design schools to offer a graduate degree in comic art.

MINNEAPOLIS COLLEGE
OF ART AND DESIGN

LOL!

Twin Cities Laughs

Go ahead and laugh! Here are some jokes about the Twin Cities to tickle your funny bone.

Where in Minneapolis can you hear water laughing?

Minnehaha Falls

New York is the Big Apple . . .

and St. Paul's neighbor is Mini-Apple!

Why shouldn't you joke around on a frozen Twin Cities lake?

It might crack up.

What is the most popular beverage in the Twin Cities?

A mini-soda

What did the Minnesota River say to the Mississippi River?

Let's meet around the bend.

Which ballpark do you need to aim for?

Target Field

What animal is always at a Minnesota Twins game?

A bat

What do dogs from Minnesota say?

Woof-dah!

What falls every winter in the Twin Cities but doesn't get hurt?

Snow

It's Alive! Animals in the Twin Cities

With its many parks and nature areas, the Twin Cities is rich with wildlife. Here are just some of animals that call the Twin Cities home.

Skunks

Gray squirrels

Northern cardinals

Painted turtles

White-tailed deer

Red foxes

The Raptor Center

The Raptor Center is for the birds. Birds of prey, that is. Its clinic at the University of Minnesota takes care of about 1,000 injured and ill raptors every year. The center's patients include eagles, kestrels, hawks, owls, and falcons. Visitors to the Raptor Center can see birds up close, explore their habitats, and learn how to protect them.

It's Alive! Animals in the Twin Cities

Some amazing wildlife lives around lakes, rivers, and streams in the Twin Cities. Check out just a few here!

Minks

Beavers

Walleye

Mallard ducks

Northern pike

River Otters

Looney Tunes!

Common loons love lakes. They spend their days floating, swimming, and diving. A loon calling out across a lake is the sound of summer for many Minnesotans. Loons make four different sounds. They laugh when alarmed. They wail to find each other. Parents hoot to each other about their young. And males yodel to protect their territory.

We Saw It at the Zoo

Como Park Zoo opened in 1897 with three deer. Today, it features animals from all over the world and is the most popular destination in St. Paul. There's so much to see! Check out gorillas, giraffes, wolves, and tigers. Don't miss Sparky the sea lion, the zoo's ambassador—he puts on a great show. In the tropical area, look for the green anaconda and the slow-moving sloth. The cold-weather area is the place to see arctic foxes, reindeer, and snow leopards. It's also where polar bears swim and play!

Giraffes

Sumatran orangutans

Polar bears

Minnesota Zoo

Opened in 1978, the Minnesota Zoo is a quick drive south of Minneapolis and St. Paul. It is home to more than 4,500 animals made up of 505 species. That's a lot of critters! And with several miles of trails, every visit to the zoo can be a different adventure. The Tropics Trail winds through a lush, green rain forest where lemurs play and gibbons hang from branches. The Northern Trail features moose, caribou, bison, and Amur tigers. Check out ocean life at Discovery Bay, home to stingrays, leopard sharks, and seals. And don't miss the penguins and snow monkeys—these favorites have their own spaces.

The Minnesota Zoo has its own farm, too. When spring arrives, so do the baby farm animals! Everyone is invited to meet and greet the newborn piglets, calves, chicks, and kids. There are even baby llamas (which are called "crias").

Bald eagle

Goat

Grizzly bear

Favorite Buildings

Minneapolis and St. Paul each have their own history and personality. And it shows in some amazing buildings. Some you've seen already . . . flip back and see!

St. Paul

Cathedral of St. Paul, 1915: A massive granite church that stands on a hill overlooking the city of St. Paul.

Landmark Center, 1902: Built as a federal courthouse and post office, it is now a cultural center for music, dance, and theater.

Union Depot, 1926: A transportation hub that is also a setting for public events, concerts, and festivals.

IDS Center, 1972: The tallest skyscraper in Minneapolis, it houses the Crystal Court, a sprawling indoor urban park.

Minneapolis City Hall, 1906: Built of rose quartz quarried in Minnesota and known for its tower with four-faced chiming clocks.

Minneapolis

Basilica of St. Mary, 1914: The first Catholic basilica in the United States.

U.S. Bank Stadium, 2016: Home of the Minnesota Vikings, the design is inspired by ice formations and longboats used long ago by Scandinavian Vikings.

Spooky Sights

Are ghosts real? No one knows for sure. But a lot of people have stories to tell of unexplained sights and sounds. Here are just a few places in the Twin Cities that might be haunted.

Let's dance! Years ago, a woman in a green coat died on the site of what is now Minneapolis's legendary music club **First Avenue**. She is said to haunt the bathroom, and staffers often see her dancing without legs. Other legless spirits sometimes join her on the dance floor. Equipment sometimes falls off stage for no reason, and deejays report hearing strange sounds and voices through their headphones. Spooky!

Are there spirits in the store? A **Dairy Queen** near a Minneapolis shopping center is thought to be haunted by young spirits from a nearby graveyard. They've been heard laughing as they knock items off shelves in closed freezers. And sometimes they print out receipts for "phantom" orders that don't exist.

Are there phantoms in the mansion? **Griggs Mansion**, which dates to the 1880s, has been called the most haunted house in St. Paul. Over the years, residents have reported unexplained sounds of footsteps, coughs, and doors closing. They have experienced a feeling of dread in the hall where a young maid died. Art students felt someone peering over their shoulders as they painted. Other residents have seen a thin man in a dark suit who then faded away.

Built in 1922, St. Paul's **Mounds Theatre** is historic, but is it also haunted? Three spirits are said to roam the place, but the most famous is a girl in a pink dress. She's often seen on stage bouncing a ball.

Festivals!

With hundreds of festivals, the Twin Cities knows how to celebrate. Here are some of the biggest festivals that everyone looks forward to!

St. Paul Winter Carnival

Time to embrace the cold! Started in 1886, the St. Paul Winter Carnival is the country's oldest winter festival. The Grande Day Parade, led by King Boreas and the Queen of the Snows, kicks off the celebration in late January. Favorite events include an ice-fishing tournament, ice-carving competition, and snow-sculpting contest. The carnival closes with a torchlight parade featuring the fire king Vulcanus Rex.

FAST FACT

According to legend, King Boreas and the Queen of the Snows reign over the St. Paul Winter Carnival. But on its tenth day, the fire king Vulcanus Rex and his Krewe overthrow King Boreas to bring summer back to the city. The king and queen must say farewell to St. Paul until the cold arrives again the next year.

Minnesota State Fair

When summer winds down, the fun heats up! The end of August brings the state fair, also known as the "Great Minnesota Get Together." Some people come just for the food, including fried cheese curds, foot-long hot dogs, and roasted sweet corn. The Giant Slide is a huge attraction. Exhibits feature farm animals, butter sculptures, and farm equipment. For great views of the fairgrounds, hop on a Skyride gondola or zoom up the Space Tower. Head to the Midway to play games and take a ride on the Great Big Wheel. At night, the Grandstand features big-name musicians.

Minneapolis Aquatennial

Minneapolis has celebrated "The 10 Best Days of Summer" for more than 80 years! Held the third week of July, the Aquatennial invites everyone to join in the fun. Milk carton boat races, sand castle contests, beach volleyball, and a triathlon are just a few popular events. Highlights include a torchlight parade and one of the country's biggest fireworks displays!

Not Far Away

There's more to explore beyond Minneapolis and St. Paul. Here are some great attractions to see on a day away.

Guess where we are: It has a rollercoaster and sharks.

Amusement park?

Nope. It has a mirror maze and mini-golf.

Super-cool game center?

Nuh-uh. Giveaway clue: It is packed with places to buy things.

OMG! A shopping mall!

Not just any mall—the **Mall of America**, south of The Cities. It's the most famous mall in the U.S. and has so much more than shopping!

Going up . . . up north, that is!

Wow! Where are you?

We took a trip north to **Duluth**. There's a lot to do here!

Tell me the truth about Duluth!

There's a cool aquarium, and a great hiking trail on Lake Superior.

Now THAT'S a Great Lake!

And this cool Aerial Lift Bridge has to rise up every time a huge ship goes through.

Hey . . . going up again!

Sister Cities Around the World

The Twin Cities are "twins," but they also have a bunch of sisters. How can that be? Minneapolis and St. Paul are each officially connected with different cities around the world. Their close relationships make them sister cities!

After World War II, the U.S. government looked for ways to keep the peace around the world. One idea was to create partnerships between cities. This idea led to the Sister Cities program, which began in 1956.

Sister Cities in Action

Here are some examples of how the Twin Cities are working with and helping their sister cities:

St. Paul and Nagasaki, Japan: Over 65 years of friendship, the two cities have exchanged letters, books, and art exhibits. St. Paul helped establish a boys' baseball team in Nagasaki. Nagasaki architects helped design the Japanese Garden in Como Park. Symphony orchestras in the two cities combined their talents. The two cities also supported ongoing student exchanges.

Minneapolis and Najaf, Iraq: Since 2009, the two cities have focused on bringing local Iraqis and non-Iraqis together. Through picnics, potlucks, and other events, the goal is to share cultures and create long-lasting friendships. Representatives from the two cities also visit each other often.

Minneapolis and Kuopio, Finland: Friends for more than 45 years, these two cities are both interested in education. Kuopio teachers visited Minneapolis teachers to share ideas. The two cities had a big book exchange, sending hundreds of books to each other. Americans visited Kuopio for their America Days festival, while the Finns came to Minnesota for FinnFest.

FIND OUT MORE!

Books, Websites, and More!

Books

Erdrich, Louise. ***The Birchbark House.*** Harper Collin's, 2021 Kindle edition.

Markovics, Joyce. ***2020 Black Lives Matter Marches.*** Cherry Lake, 2021.

Purslow, Neil. ***Minnesota.*** SmarkBook Media, 2022.

Rendon, Marcia. ***Powwow Summer.*** Minnesota Historical Society, 2013.

Whiting, Jim. ***Minnesota Vikings.*** Creative Paperbacks, 2019.

Zobel, Derek. ***Minnesota (State Profiles).*** Bellwether, 2022.

Web Sites

https://www.seattleschild.com
Activity guide for kids of all ages.

Meet Minneapolis
https://www.minneapolis.org/

Visit St. Paul
https://www.visitsaintpaul.com/

Como Park Zoo
https://comozooconservatory.org/

Explore Minnesota
https://www.exploreminnesota.com/

Minnesota History Center
https://www.mnhs.org/historycenter

MNopedia
https://www.mnopedia.org/

Photo Credits and Thanks

Photos from Dreamstime, National Archives, Library of Congress, Shutterstock, or Wikimedia unless otherwise noted. 17 top: Minnesota Historical Society; 23 top: AP Photos/Peter Southwick; 61 bottom: AP Photo/Jeff Roberson; 45 bottom: Glen Stubbe/Zuma Press/Newscom. 50 top: Science Museum of Minnesota.

Artwork: Shutterstock: LemonadePixel. Maps (6-7): Jessica Nevins.

Thanks to our pal Nancy Ellwood and the fine folks at Arcadia!

INDEX

Thanks for Visiting

The TWIN CITIES

Come Back Soon!